If someone said, "Our son is really hot today," what picture would come into your mind? A sweating boy? Our nearest star? If you couldn't see "son" spelled s-o-n, you might think it was "sun" spelled s-u-n because those words sound exactly alike. But they have different spellings and meanings. In fact, the spelling helps us know the meaning of the word. These words are called homophones and can be a bit tricky. But let's have some fun with them. Here's the game.

On each right-hand page, you'll see a sentence with a homophone in it. Think of a different sentence that sounds exactly the same, but with the homophone changed into its sound-alike partner. For example, you might replace "son" with "sun" and think of how you would draw a picture to show what that sentence means.

Then turn the page, and you'll see a version of that second sentence. If the sentence you thought of is different, you can draw it on a piece of paper and stick it into this book. Challenge your friends to make up their own second sentences. See who comes up with the funniest or weirdest ones.

Ready? Let's play!

Measure the **FLOUR**.

Measure the FLOWER.

This is the longest **TALE** we've ever seen.

This is the longest TAIL we've ever seen.

It was the biggest **SALE** ever!

It was the biggest SAIL ever!

You'll love this new **CENT**.

You'll love this new SCENT.

It's CHILLY!

It's CHILI!

A loud CREAK startled him.

A loud **CREEK** startled him.

I have many **HAIRS**.

I have many **HARES**.

HEY!

HAY!

What a **WASTE**!

What a **WAIST**!

I'll take those **PEARS**.

I'll take those **PAIRS**.

Wash off your **PRINTS**.

Wash off your PRINCE.

Follow this **ROOT**.

Follow this **ROUTE**.

The COLONEL exploded.

The KERNEL exploded.

Spray all your ANTS.

Spray all your AUNTS.

Now we knead the DOUGH.

Now we need the DOE.

He's in GREECE.

He's in GREASE.

She's wearing over 50 CARATS!

She's wearing over 50 CARROTS!

This will fix the PAIN.

This will fix the **PANE**.

When you need a **TOW**, call us.

When you need a **TOE**, call us.

Our SON is very hot today.

Our SUN is very hot today.

What's the Difference?

Homonyms: two or more words that have the same spelling or pronunciation but different meanings. Both homophones and homographs are types of homonyms.

Homophones: two or more words that sound the same but have different meanings (For example: they're, their, there.)

Homographs: two or more words that are spelled the same but have different meanings (For example, bark on a tree and a dog's bark.)

Now try making up your own fun sentences with these pairs of homonyms.

add ad	flea flee	plain plane
ate eight	flu flue	poll pole
bare bear	heal heel	poor pour
beat beet	hi high	right write
blew blue	hoarse horse	rose rows
boarder border	hoes hose	sea see
bow beau	knot not	sew so
cell sell	made maid	stair stare
crews cruise	mail male	steal steel
dear deer	meat meet	time thyme
days daze	night knight	wail whale
eye I	oar or	way weigh
fare fair	one won	weak week
feat feet	pail pale	which witch
firs furs	peace piece	yokes yolks

Marvin Terban

is a popular, best-selling children's book author and a long-time educator. Called a "master of children's wordplay" by ALA Booklist and "Mr. English for Kids" by the Children's Book-of-the-Month Club, he has written 40 books for young readers, most of them about the English language. He is also Scholastic's "Professor Grammar." Marvin Terban has been teaching English, Latin, and other subjects at Columbia Grammar and Preparatory School in New York City for 60 years.

Andreas Wittmann

As a small child, Andreas fell into a large pot of paint. From that day on, he loved to draw. Later, he studied art at the Academy of Fine Arts in Munich. Now he is an illustrator and art teacher. He lives with his wife and their two children in an old house with a wild garden, where he grows carrots for rabbit clothes.